THE BLACK NORTH
IN 1901

A SOCIAL STUDY

A Series of Articles Originally Appearing in
The New York Times, November-December 1901

W. E. Burghardt Du Bois

ARNO PRESS and THE NEW YORK TIMES
NEW YORK 1969

General Editor
WILLIAM LOREN KATZ

THE BLACK NORTH IN 1901

On the day before the young and optimistic Martin Luth-
er King spoke so passionately and eloquently of "The
Dream" to the vast interracial throng assembled before
the Lincoln Memorial during the summer of 1963, another great Afro-American died in self-exile at the age of
ninety-five. He had joined the American Communist
Party in 1961 to the surprise and dismay of thousands
of his friends and admirers, and then emigrated to Ghana
in West Africa and renounced his American citizenship.
Yet, the passing of Dr. W. E. B. Du Bois could not be
ignored by those who had assembled to reaffirm their
own faith in the promise of American democracy, for
the leaders on the platform all knew that without him
they would not have been there. In the early years of
the century, when the status of black men and women
in the United States was at what Professor Rayford Logan
has called "the nadir," Du Bois had urged the nation to
return to the spirit of John Brown and had organized a
group of Negro intellectuals into the Niagara Movement.
Some of these black militants later formed a coalition
with white liberals and socialists that became, in 1909,
the National Association for the Advancement of Colored
People (NAACP). Dr. Du Bois edited its journal, *The Crisis*, for twenty-five years. So, when word of his death
came, the leaders of the March on Washington paid brief
tribute to the pioneer and then turned to the pressing
business of that historic day, the demand for something

expressed on many of the placards: JOBS AND FREE-
DOM.

As uncomfortable as the memory of him is, America
cannot forget Dr. Du Bois, the first, and, perhaps, still,
the greatest of the black scholars she has produced.
Trained at Fisk and Harvard, and seasoned in German
universities, his superb mind was unusually productive.
The Souls of Black Folk; *Black Reconstruction*; *Black
Folks Then, and Now*; *Dusk of Dawn*; *The World and
Africa*; and his posthumous autobiography confront us on
the shelves of libraries and bookstores. Any definitive bib-
liography on "The Negro" will include these and others
of the twenty-one books and ninety-nine pamphlets, es-
says and articles that he published, as well as fifteen vol-
umes of the proceedings of the Annual Conference on
the Negro Problem, at Atlanta University, which he organized. We are forced to ask ourselves an embarrassing
question: "Why, just before his death, did Dr. Du Bois
repudiate the land of his birth?" No easy answer can be
given, for he was a very complex person — brilliant, sensitive, continuously striving to relate his action to new
intellectual insights, and considered "difficult" by some
of his more pedestrian and less flexible associates.

Basically, however, Dr. Du Bois's "defection" was an
expression of impatience with what he considered an un-
forgivably slow rate of change in the status of black men
in America during a period when the winds of change
were blowing with revolutionary velocity elsewhere. During his long life he had seen much and suffered much —
directly and vicariously — wars, panics, depressions, and
race riots. His "Litany of Atlanta," written after he and
his family had lived through a race riot in 1906, was a

poetic cry of rage that preceded his decision to return to the North where he began his life. Born in Massachusetts three years after the Civil War, Du Bois was almost fifty when "Make the World Safe for Democracy" became the national war-cry. By the time the "War Against Facism" was fought, he was in his seventies.

Du Bois was eighty-six when the Supreme Court decision of 1954 repudiated the doctrine of "Separate but Equal" and signalled the opening of the Desegregation Decade. He witnessed massive southern resistance to what was advertised as a national commitment, and reflected upon the dramatic upsurge of the Negro middle-class and educated youth in the Civil Rights Movement against that resistance — non-violent in form, but receiving occasional, though very limited, applications of federal power to re-inforce it. He conceded, in his *Autobiography*, that *some* significant changes were taking place in the South, but as hard as he, himself, had fought in the past for civil rights and desegregation, he did not think advances in these areas touched the basic problems of the black masses in either the North or the South. And, even the limited gains were menaced by the dreaded prospect of a possible nuclear war. To act with conviction on the twin issues of poverty and war during the McCarthy Era was to risk the label of "subversive," so he found himself under federal indictment as he reached his eightieth birthday. Bitterness and disillusionment, as well as ideology, entered into his final fateful decisions.

Du Bois's preoccupation with the economic problems of black men in the United States, over and above his concern for their civil liberties, was not an aberration of his old age. In fact, he was virtually forced to sever his

connection with the NAACP during the Depression when
that organization could not sanction his use of the col-
umns of *The Crisis* to call for a type of economic mobili-
zation that, to an interracial board committed to "inte-
gration," seemed suspiciously close to "black separatism."
He was calling for a buying club or cooperative store in
every ghetto church, and for black people to "buy black"
in order to provide employment for their unemployed.
This concentration upon economic matters was the out-
come of a line of thought that began much earlier and
found expression in a series of five articles written for
The New York Times in 1901 on "The Black North."
Although a professor at Atlanta University in the Deep
South, Dr. Du Bois was still reflecting upon the field-work
he had done a few years earlier that had produced a clas-
sic in American sociology, *The Philadelphia Negro*, and
he had presided over conferences between 1897 and 1900,
whose proceedings were published as *Social and Physical
Conditions of Negroes in Cities*, *Some Efforts of American Negroes for Their Own Social Betterment*, and *The
Negro in Business*.

The opening words of the series reveal dramatic changes
in the temper of the times: "The negro (sic) problem is
not the sole property of the South. To be sure it is there
most complicated and pressing." Both sociologists and
the media, today, define "white racism" and not "the
Negro" as the problem; and, also, sometime during the
1930's, *The New York Times* led the way in adjustment
to Negro demands for a capital "N." Now, "black" is in
semantic vogue. The urban North has replaced the South
as the problem focus, for the "hot summers" that began
in Philadelphia, New York, and Rochester in 1964, have

burned the fact into our minds that the vast northern ghettos are the testing ground of the nation's ability to realize its democratic values. But Du Bois's assessment of the underlying causes of ghetto social disorganization and black discontent are as relevant today as in 1901: "The problem of work, the problem of poverty, is today the central baffling problem of the Northern negro." That these had remained the key problems for over sixty years as the nation moved toward affluence was an important factor in Du Bois's rejection of the American social system. In his eyes, despite considerable "improvement" in the status of Negroes, nothing in New York, Philadelphia, Boston, or other northern cities had *really* changed since he wrote in 1901. Readers now have an opportunity to make the comparison for themselves.

Du Bois summarized his field-research on Philadelphia and assembled statistical data and survey materials for New York and Boston. He rated the cities from "better" to "worst," with Boston presenting the most favorable situation for Negroes and New York the least. In each case, he also presented a short historical sketch to remind his readers that these black communities were very old, and that segregation and discrimination had been present from the beginning. He was impressed by the fact that they had survived at all in view of predictions that had been made that high death and disease rates would eventually eliminate them. And, he depicted the processes by which, in New York and Philadelphia, their economic strangulation was attempted by foreign-born economic competitors through race riot and union restrictions. Yet, Du Bois felt that the black communities had paid a high price for survival — the constant inflow of migrants from the South, less literate than the existing population, "rougher" in manners and morals, and with more women than men among them, thus exhibiting all the problems that flow from an unbalanced sex ratio. Many northern black communities were "periodically overwhelmed" and earlier settlers were "dragged back by a mass of immigrants." Boston, on the other hand, had a measure of demographic stability that was reflected in lower crime rates and a more orderly population. He drove home the point that "in-migration" was related to demands for labor, but that once Negroes were in the city an attempt was made to confine them to the most menial types of jobs. Boston had achieved the most balanced occupational structure, but even here mobility to the "top" had never been achieved. (Reflecting upon what Du Bois had to say about Massachusetts, in general, and Boston in particular, the possibility of electing a Negro state senator years later might have been predicted.)

The changes that sixty years wrought in Du Bois, himself, as he reflected upon poverty and racial discrimination and their social consequences, can be measured by using these articles as a baseline. Here is deep concern for the welfare of the poor — black and white — something that remained a constant throughout his life. His basic analysis of the social forces that gave black poverty its special character underwent little change, but his conception of what the black poor should do about their plight changed markedly. The articles indict a social system that bred poverty and bore down with extra weight upon Negroes due to the racism institutionalized within it, but the solutions to the problem were seen in terms of a constant individual struggle to shake off apathy and lethargy, to cultivate sobriety, decorous law-abiding behavior, and conventional sexual behavior, and above all skill and competence in work. Measurement of racial progress was cited in terms of proportions of people who had moved into "better" jobs as the years passed and in a decline in crime rates.

The socio-economic strata among Philadelphia Negroes were defined as: "the aristocracy of wealth and education," "the hard-working poor," "the poor and unfortunate," and "the Submerged Tenth" — "social failures" characterized by "debauchery and crime" and given to "excess and immorality." In New York, Du Bois also saw too many "criminals and loafers . . . encouraged and protected by political corruption and race prejudice." Even in Boston, which was a model of racial stability and adjustment, there was the "usual substratum of crime and idleness," though much smaller in proportion than in the other two cities. The "social failures" were responsible for the stereotyped "characteristics" of black people that made it easier for whites to justify their prejudice and discrimination, and they were a menace to middle-class Negroes. The situation in Boston was healthier because as Negroes moved *up* they could also move *out*, housing discrimination being less rigid there. Du Bois said that all three situations demanded "systematic search for work," "better homes" and "political reform," and "the home training of children should be more strict even than that of whites." He felt that "social distinctions should be observed. A rising race must be aristocratic; the good cannot consort with the bad, nor even the best with the less good." Du Bois in 1901 sounded like any white social worker or philanthropist.

Written eight years before the founding of the NAACP, these articles could as easily have borne the signature of Booker T. Washington as of Du Bois. But the sociologist in Du Bois eventually prevailed over the moralist. He came to see institutional racism as a factor that set limits upon the number and proportion of black people who could ever rise out of the two bottom social categories he had defined. Before World War I broke out, he had left the moralizing and the exhortations to "build better mouse-traps" to preachers, school teachers, and followers, generally, of Booker T. Washington. In the racial division of labor he took on another task, leading the fight to alter the social structure so as to expand opportunities for black men. The small size of these communities (60,000 Negroes each in New York and Philadelphia, and 12,000 in Boston) and their powerlessness were undoubtedly factors that led Du Bois to stress the acquisition of middle-class virtues and the need to win the favor of the white wielders of power and influence. But, also, Du Bois was still basically a New England aristocrat at heart.

In a very perceptive comment on the Philadelphia "aristocracy of wealth and education," however, he isolated a "paradox":

> ... not being to any extent themselves employers of colored labor or bound to them by ties of industrial interest they cannot assume control over their own people. Indeed, a natural instinct of self-preservation drives them away from the lower masses of their people. They feel they can only maintain their position and advance further by drawing social lines against the incompetent and criminal of their own race. Thus they face a peculiar paradox and stand between black and white, the representatives of all that is best in the one

and at the same time suffering vicariously at the hands of
the other for all that is worst among their own people.

By 1935, he had resolved the paradox for himself by
making an intellectual commitment to devising plans by
which those "masses" could be organized and led by Negroes of higher status within the framework of a cooperative movement. By then, the population base of all three
communities had been expanded by massive migrations
from the South and new perspectives had opened up.
Du Bois, like most Negro leaders, was thinking now in
terms of how "Black Power" could be mobilized so that
Negroes could shape their own destiny. All the leaders
remained "upper class" and "upper middle-class" in their
own styles of life, but saw their roles as supplying leadership to the "masses." Negroes won considerable political power, but remained economically powerless. No
cooperative movement for survival developed, and any
type of separate black economy seemed senseless after
the war boom of the 1940's began.

By 1960, Du Bois had decided that neither Black Cap-
italism nor the cooperative movement, nor balance-of-
power politics, could deliver the final blow to racism and
poverty. He embraced "communism," insisting, however, in his *Autobiography*, upon a small "c." He then
stood alone, "alienated," for this proposed solution was
not acceptable to the black community. But his intellectual endeavors and the sincerity of his commitment
had the abiding respect and admiration of even those
who repudiated his ideology.

The publication of these articles by the "early Du Bois"
is welcomed by all students of Black History who are en-

gaged in "fleshing out" details about matters only vaguely known, and in "setting the record straight." But they have significance, too, for all concerned American citizens. They confront us with a frightening fact, that after sixty-eight years, black people are *still* paying higher rents than whites for similar accommodations; that most whites *still* refuse to accept them as neighbors; that they are *still* subject to the hostility of the foreign-born and their children; that unions *still* seek to bar them; and that though the level at which the "poverty line" is set is higher than it was in 1901, blacks *still* make up from a quarter to a third of those defined as "poor" in northern cities.

If reflection upon the persistence of these conditions drove one sensitive black man, in his old age, to despair of any solution short of a revolutionary restructuring of American society, what can we expect from the tens of thousands of angry young black men today, as they grow older in *their* impatience? Du Bois felt in 1901 as responsible black leaders feel now, and ended his series of articles with a query: "Is it necessary in the twentieth century to point out so plain a duty to fair-minded Americans?"

St. Clair Drake
PROFESSOR OF SOCIOLOGY AND ANTHROPOLOGY
ROOSEVELT UNIVERSITY

NEW YORK CITY
PART I

The negro problem is not the sole property of the South. To be sure, it is there most complicated and pressing. Yet north of Mason and Dixon's line there live to-day three-quarters of a million men of negro lineage. Nearly 400,000 of these live in New England and the Middle Atlantic States, and it is this population that I wish especially to study in a series of papers.

The growth of this body of negroes has been rapid since the war. There were 150,000 in 1860, 225,000 in 1880, and about 385,000 to-day. It is usually assumed that this group of persons has not formed to any extent a "problem" in the North, that during a century of freedom they have had an assured social status and the same chance for rise and development as the native white American, or at least as the foreign immigrant.

This is not true. It can be safely asserted that since early Colonial times the North has had a distinct race problem. Every one of these States had slaves, and at the beginning of Washington's Administration there were 40,000 black slaves and 17,000 black freemen in this section. The economic failure of slavery as an investment here gave the better conscience of Puritan and Quaker a chance to be heard, and processes of gradual emancipation were begun early in the nineteenth century.

Some of the slaves were sold South and eagerly welcomed there. Most of them stayed in the North and became a free negro population.

1

They were not, however, really free. Socially they were ostracized. Strict laws were enacted against inter-marriage. They were granted rights of suffrage with some limitations, but these limitations were either increased or the right summarily denied afterward.

North as well as South the negroes have emerged from slavery into a serfdom of poverty and restricted rights. Their history since has been the history of the gradual but by no means complete breaking down of remaining barriers.

To-day there are many contrasts between Northern and Southern negroes. Three-fourths of the Southern negroes live in the country districts. Nine-tenths of the Northern negroes live in cities and towns. The Southern negroes were in nearly all cases born South and of slave parentage.

About a third of the Northern negroes were born North, partly of free negro parentage, while the rest are Southern immigrants. Thus in the North there is a sharp-er division of the negroes into classes and a greater differ-ence in attainment and training than one finds in the South.

From the beginning the Northern slaves lived in towns more generally than the Southern slaves, being used large-ly as house servants and artisans. As town life increased, the urban negro population increased. Here and there little villages of free negroes were to be found in the country districts of the North tilling the soil, but the competition of the great West soon sent them to town along with their white brothers, and now only here and there is there a negro family left in the country districts and villages of New England and of the Middle States.

From the earliest settlement of Manhattan, when the Dutch West India Company was pledging itself to furnish the new settlers with plenty of negroes, down to 1900, when the greater city contained 60,000 black folk, New York has had a negro problem. This problem has greatly changed from time to time. Two centuries ago it was a question of obtaining "hands" to labor. Then came questions of curbing barbarians and baptizing heathen. Long before the nineteenth century citizens were puzzled about the education of negroes, and then came negro riots and negro crime and the baffling windings of the color line.

At the beginning of the eighteenth century there were 1,500 negroes in New York City. They were house servants and laborers, and often were hired out by their masters, taking their stand for this purpose at the foot of Wall Street. By the middle of the century the population had doubled, and by the beginning of the nineteenth century it was about 9,000, five-sixths of whom were free by the act of gradual emancipation.

In 1840 the population was over 16,000, but it fell off to 12,500 in 1860 on account of the competition of foreign workmen and race riots. Since the war it has increased rapidly to 20,000 in 1880 and to 36,000 on Manhattan Island in 1900. The annexed districts raise this total to 60,666 for the whole city.

The distribution of this population presents many curious features. Conceive a large rectangle through which Seventh Avenue runs lengthwise. Let this be bounded on the south by a line near Sixteenth Street and on the north by Sixty-fourth or Sixty-fifth Street. On the east let the boundary be a wavering line between Fourth and Seventh Avenues and on the west the river.

In this quadrangle live over 20,000 negroes, a third of the total population. Ten thousand others live around the north end of the Park and further north, while 18,000 live in Brooklyn. The remaining 10,000 are scattered here and there in other parts of the city.

The migration of the black population to its present abode in New York has followed the growth of the city. Early in the eighteenth century negroes lived and congregated in the hovels along the wharves and of course in the families of the masters. The centre of black population then moved slowly north, principally on the east side, until it reached Mulberry Street, about 1820. Crossing Broadway, a generation later the negroes clustered about Sullivan and Thompson Streets until after the war, when they moved northward along Seventh Avenue.

From 1870 to 1890 the population was more and more crowded and congested in the negro districts between Twenty-sixth and Sixty-third Streets. Since then there has been considerable dispersion to Brooklyn and the Harlem districts, although the old centres are still full.

The migration to Brooklyn began about 1820 and received its great impetus from the refugees at the time of the draft riots. In 1870 there were 5,000 negroes in Brooklyn. Since then the population has increased very rapidly, and it has consisted largely of the better class of negroes in search of homes and seeking to escape the contamination of the Tenderloin.

In 1890 the Brooklyn negroes had settled chiefly in the Eleventh, Twentieth, and Seventh Wards. Since then they have increased in those wards and have moved to the east in the Twenty-third, Twenty-fourth, and Twenty-fifth Wards and in the vicinity of Coney Island.

Let us now examine any peculiarities in the colored population of Greater New York. The first noticeable fact is the excess of women. In Philadelphia the women exceed the men six to five. In New York the excess is still larger—five to four—and this means that here even more than in Philadelphia the demand for negro housemaids is unbalanced by a corresponding demand for negro men.

This disproportion acts disastrously to-day on the women and the men. The excess of young people from eighteen to thirty years of age points again to large and rapid immigration. The Wilmington riot alone sent North thousands of emigrants, and as the black masses of the South awaken or as they are disturbed by the violence this migration will continue and perhaps increase.

The North, therefore, and especially great cities like New York, has much more than an academic interest in the Southern negro problem. Unless the race conflict there is so adjusted as to leave the negroes a contented, industrious people, they are going to migrate here and there. And into the large cities will pour in increasing numbers the competent and the incompetent, the industrious and the lazy, the law abiding and the criminal.

Moreover, the conditions under which these new immigrants are now received are of such a nature that very frequently the good are made bad and the bad made professional criminals. One has but to read Dunbar's "Sport of the Gods" to get an idea of the temptations that surround the young immigrant. In the most thickly settled negro portion of the Nineteenth Assembly District, where 5,000 negroes live, the parents of half of the heads of families were country bred. Among these families the strain of city life is immediately seen when we find that 24 per cent. of the mothers are widows—a percentage only exceeded by the Irish, and far above the Americans, (16.3.)

In these figures lie untold tales of struggle, self-denial, despair, and crime. In the country districts of the South, as in all rural regions, early marriage and large families are the rule. These young immigrants to New York cannot afford to marry early. Two-thirds of the young men twenty to twenty-four years of age are unmarried, and five-eighths of the young women.

When they do marry it is a hard struggle to earn a living. As a race the negroes are not lazy. The canvass of the Federation of Churches in typical New York tenement districts has shown that while nearly 99 per cent. of the black men were wage earners, only 92 per cent. of the Americans and 90 per cent. of the Germans were at work.

At the same time the work of the negroes was least remunerative, they receiving a third less per week than the other nationalities. Nor can the disabilities of the negroes be laid altogether at the door of ignorance. Probably they are even less acquainted with city life and organized industry than most of the foreign laborers. In illiteracy, however, negroes and foreigners are about equal —five-sixths being able to read and write.

The crucial question, then, is: What does the black immigrant find to do? Some persons deem the answer to this question unnecessary to a real understanding of the negro. They say either that the case of the negro is that of the replacing of a poor workman by better ones in the natural competition of trade or that a mass of people

like the American negroes ought to furnish employment
for themselves without asking others for work.

There is just enough truth in such superficial state-
ments to make them peculiarly misleading and unfair.
Before the civil war the negro was certainly as efficient a
workman as the raw immigrant from Ireland or Germany.
But whereas the Irishmen found economic opportunity
wide and daily growing wider, the negro found public
opinion determined to "keep him in his place."

As early as 1824 Lafayette, on his second visit to New
York, remarked "with astonishment the aggravation of
the prejudice against the blacks," and stated that in the
Revolutionary War "the black and white soldiers messed
together without hesitation." In 1836 a well-to-do negro
was refused a license as a drayman in New York City, and
mob violence was frequent against black men who pushed
forward beyond their customary sphere.

Nor could the negro resent this by his vote. The Con-
stitution of 1777 had given him full rights of suffrage,
but in 1821 the ballot, so far as blacks were concerned,
was restricted to holders of $250 worth of realty—a re-
striction which lasted until the war, in spite of efforts to
change it, and which restricted black laborers but left
white laborers with full rights of suffrage.

So, too, the draft riots of 1863 were far more than
passing ebullitions of wrath and violence, but were used
as a means of excluding negroes all over the city from
lines of work in which they had long been employed.
The relief committee pleaded in vain to have various positions restored to negroes. In numerous cases the exclusion
was permanent and remains so to this day.

Thus the candid observer easily sees that the negro's

economic position in New York has not been determined
simply by efficiency in open competition, but that race
prejudice has played a large and decisive part. Probably
in free competition ex-slaves would have suffered some
disadvantages in entering mechanical industries. When
race feeling was added to this they were almost totally
excluded.

Again, it is impossible for a group of men to maintain
and employ itself while in open competition with a larger
and stronger group. Only by co-operation with the industrial organization of the Nation can negroes earn a
living. And this co-operation is difficult to effect. One
can easily trace the struggle in a city like New York.
Seventy-four per cent. of the working negro population
are common laborers and servants.

From this dead level they have striven long to rise. In
this striving they have made many mistakes, have had
some failures and some successes. They voluntarily withdrew from bootblacking, barbering, table waiting, and
menial service whenever they thought they saw a chance
to climb higher, and their places were quickly filled by
foreign whites.

Some of the negroes succeeded in their efforts to rise,
some did not. Thus every obstacle placed in the way of
their progress meant increased competition at the bottom.
Twenty-six per cent. of the negroes have risen to a degree
and gained a firmer economic foothold. Twelve per cent.
of these have gone but a step higher; these are the porters,
packers, messengers, draymen, and the like—a select class
of laborers, often well paid and more independent than
the old class of upper house servants before the war, to
which they in some respects correspond.

Some of this class occupy responsible positions, others have some capital invested, and nearly all have good homes.

Ten per cent. of the colored people are skilled laborers —cigarmakers, barbers, tailors and dressmakers, builders, stationary engineers, &c. Five and one-half per cent. are in business enterprises of various sorts. The negroes have something over a million and a half dollars invested in small business enterprises, chiefly real estate, the catering business, undertaking, drug stores, hotels and restaurants, express teaming, &c. In the sixty-nine leading establishments $800,000 is invested—$13,000 in sums from $500 to $1,000 and $269,000 in sums from $1,000 to $25,000.

Forty-four of the sixty-nine businesses were established since 1885, and seventeen others since the war. Co-operative holders of real estate—i.e., hall associations, building and loan associations, and one large church, which has considerable sums in productive real estate—have over half a million dollars invested. Five leading caterers have $30,000, seven undertakers have $32,000, two saloons have over $50,000, and four small machine shops have $27,500 invested.

These are the most promising enterprises in which New York negroes have embarked. Serious obstacles are encountered. Great ingenuity is often required in finding gaps in business service where the man of small capital may use his skill or experience.

One negro has organized the cleaning of houses to a remarkable extent and has an establishment representing at least $20,000 of invested capital, some ten or twelve employes, and a large circle of clients.

Again, it is very difficult for negroes to get experience and training in modern business methods. Young colored men can seldom get positions above menial grade, and the training of the older men unfits them for competitive business. Then always the uncertain but ever present factor of racial prejudice is present to hinder or at least make more difficult the advance of the colored merchant or business man, in new or unaccustomed lines.

In clerical and professional work there are about ten negro lawyers in New York, twenty physicians, and at least ninety in the civil service as clerks, mail carriers, public school teachers, and the like. The competitive civil service has proved a great boon to young aspiring negroes, and they are being attracted to it in increasing numbers. Already in the public schools there are one Principal, two special teachers, and about thirty-five class-room teachers of negro blood. So far no complaint of the work and very little objection to their presence has been heard.

In some such way as this black New York seeks to earn its daily bread, and it remains for us to ask of the homes and the public institutions just what kind of success these efforts are having.

NEW YORK CITY
PART II

Taking all available data into consideration we may conclude that of the 60,000 negroes in New York about 15,000 are supported by workers who earn a good living in vocations above domestic service and common labor. Some thirty thousand are kept above actual want by the wages of servants and day laborers. This leaves a great struggling, unsuccessful substratum of 15,000, including "God's poor, the devil's poor, and the poor devils," and, also, the vicious and criminal classes. These are not all paupers or scamps, but they form that mass of men who through their own fault or through the fault of conditions about them have not yet succeeded in successfully standing the competition of a great city.

Such figures are of course largely conjectural, but they appear near the truth. So large a substratum of unsuccessful persons in a community is abnormal and dangerous. And yet it is certain that nothing could be more disgraceful than for New York to condemn 45,000 hard working and successful people, who have struggled up in spite of slavery, riot, and discrimination, on account of 15,000 who have not yet succeeded and whom New Yorkers have helped to fail.

In no better way can one see the effects of color prejudice on the mass of the negroes than by studying their homes. The work of the Federation of Churches in the Eleventh and Thirteenth Assembly Districts, where over 6,000 negroes live, found 19 per cent. living in one and

11

two room tenements, 37 per cent. in three rooms, and 44 per cent. in four or more rooms. Had the rooms been of good size and the rents fair this would be a good showing; but 400 of the rooms had no access to the outer air and 655 had but one window. Moreover, for these accommodations the negroes pay from $1 to $2 a month more than the whites for similar tenements—an excess rent charge which must amount to a quarter of a million dollars annually throughout the city. One fourth of these people paid under $10 a month rent; two-thirds paid from $10 to $20.

We may say, then, that in the Tenderloin district, where the newer negro immigrants must needs go for a home, the average family occupies three small rooms, for which it pays $10 to $15 a month. If the family desires a home further from the vice and dirt of New York's most dangerous slum, it must go either to Brooklyn or, far from work, up town, or be prepared to pay exorbitant rents in the vicinity of Fifty-third Street.

More than likely the new-comer knows nothing of the peculiar dangers of this district, but takes it as part of the new and strange city life to which he has migrated. Finding work scarce and rent high, he turns for relief to narrow quarters and the lodging system. In the more crowded colored districts 40 per cent. of the families take lodgers and in only 50 per cent. of the cases are the lodgers in any way related to the families. Unknown strangers are thus admitted to the very heart of homes in order that the rent may be paid. And these homes are already weak from the hereditary influence of slavery and its attendant ills.

The very first movement of philanthropy in solving

some of the negro problems of New York would be the separation of the decent and vicious elements, which the lodging system and high rent bring in such fatal proximity. Thus the movement of the City and Suburban Homes Company to build a model negro tenement on Sixty-second Street is an act of far-seeing wisdom. To-day it is the intricate and close connection of misfortune and vice among the lower classes that baffles intelligent reform.

A great mass of people, bringing with them a host of unhealthful habits, living largely in tenements, with wretched sanitary appliances, and in poor repair—such a mass must necessarily have a higher death rate than the average among the whites. Before the war this excess was very great, and even this year the colored death rate is 28 per thousand, against 20 for the whites. Since 1870 the death rate of negroes has been:

1870, 36 per thousand.
1880, 37 per thousand.
1890, 38 per thousand.
1900, 28 per thousand.

The decrease in 1900 is due to the inclusion of the healthier negro districts of the greater city, as, e. g., Brooklyn, and the immigration of young people. In itself a death rate of 28 is not high; the death rate of the whole city was 29 in 1870. Nevertheless, the disparity between whites and blacks shows plainly that the difference is due primarily to conditions of life and is remediable.

The most sinister index of social degredation and struggle is crime. Unfortunately, it is extremely difficult to-day to measure negro crime. If we seek to measure it in the South we are confronted by the fact that different and peculiar standards of justice exist for black and white. If we take a city like New York we find that continual migration and concentration of negro population here make it unfair to attribute to the city or to the permanent negro population the crime of the new-comers. Then, again, it has been less than a generation since, even in this city, negroes stood on a different footing before the courts from whites, and received severer treatment. In interpreting figures from the past, therefore, we must allow something at least for this.

There was complaint of negro misdemeanors back in the seventeenth century, as, for example, in 1682, when the city was suffering "great inconvenyencys" from the "frequent meetings and gatherings of negroes," and the City Council passed ordinances against such disorder and gambling. There was continual fear of negro uprisings, and when, after the establishment of Nean's Negro School, in 1704, a family of seven were murdered by their slaves, a great outcry was raised against negro education.

In 1712 and 1741 there were negro conspiracies—the first a fierce dash for freedom, the second a combination of negro thieves, white women of evil repute and their aiders and abettors. The city on both these occasions was vastly scared, and took fearful vengeance on those whom they thought guilty, burning and hanging twenty-nine blacks in 1741.

No very exact data of negro crime are available until about seventy-five years ago. In 1827, 25 per cent. of the convicts in New York State were negroes, although the negroes formed but 1 per cent. of the population. Twenty years later the negroes, forming the same proportion of the population, furnished 257 of the 1,637

convicts, or more than 15 per cent. In 1870 the proportion had fallen to 6 per cent.

Since then we may use the arrests in New York City
as a crude indication of negro crime. These indicate that
from 1870 to 1885 the negroes formed about 2 per cent.
of the arrests, the best record they have had in the city.
From 1885 to 1895 the proportion rose to 2½ per cent.,
and since then it has risen to 3½ per cent. A part of this
rise is accounted for by the increase in the proportion of
negro to white population, which was 1 1-3 per cent. in
1870 and 1¾ per cent. in 1900. The larger proportion
of the increase in arrests is undoubtedly due to migration
—the sudden contact of new-comers with unknown city
life. From the mere record of arrests one can get no very
good idea of crime, and yet it is safe to conclude from
the fact that in the State in 1890 every 10,000 negroes
furnished 100 prisoners that there is much serious crime
among negroes. And, indeed, what else should we expect?

What else is this but the logical result of bad homes,
poor health, restricted opportunities for work, and general social oppression? That the present situation is abnormal all admit. That the negro under normal conditions is law-abiding and good-natured cannot be disputed.
We have but to change conditions, then, to reduce negro
crime.

We have so far a picture of the negro from without—
his numbers, his dwelling place, his work, his health, and
crime. Let us now, if possible, place ourselves within the
negro group and by studying that inner life look with
him out upon the surrounding world. When a white person comes once vividly to realize the disabilities under
which a negro labors, the public contempt and thinly

veiled private dislike, "the spurns that patient merit of the unworthy takes"—when once one sees this, and then from personal knowledge knows that sensitive human hearts are enduring this, the question comes, How can they stand it? The answer is clear and peculiar: They do not stand it; they withdraw themselves as far as possible from it into a world of their own. They live and move in a community of their own kith and kin and shrink quickly and permanently from those rough edges where contact with the larger life of the city wounds and humiliates them.

To see what this means in practice, let us follow the life of an average New York negro. He is first born to a colored father and mother. The mulattoes we see on the streets are almost invariably the descendants of one, two, or three generations of mulattoes, the infusion of white blood coming often far back in the eighteenth century. In only 3 per cent. of the New York marriages of colored people is one of the parties white. The child's neighbors, as he grows up, are colored, for he lives in a colored district. In the public school he comes into intimate touch with white children, but as they grow up public opinion forces them to discard their colored acquaintances, and they soon forget even the nod of recognition. The young man's friends and associates are therefore all negroes. When he goes to work he works alongside colored men in most cases; his social circle, his clubs and organizations throughout the city are all confined to his own race, and his contact with the whites is practically confined to economic relationships, the streets, and street cars, with occasionally some intercourse at public amusements.

The centre of negro life in New York is still the church,

although its all-inclusive influence here is less than in a
Southern city. There are thirty or forty churches, large
and small, but seven or eight chief ones. They have strong-
ly marked individuality, and stand in many cases for distinct social circles. The older families of well-to-do free
negroes who count an unspotted family life for two centuries gather at St. Philip's Episcopal Church, on Twenty-
fifth Street. This church is an offshoot of Trinity and the
lineal descendant of Nean's Negro School early in the
eighteenth century. The mass of middle-class negroes
whose fathers were New Yorkers worship at Mother Zion,
Tenth and Bleecker Streets. This church is far from the
present centre of negro population, but it is a historic
spot, where the first organized protest of black folk against color discrimination in New York churches took
place. Up on Fifty-third Street, at Olivet, one finds a
great Baptist church, with the newer immigrants from
Georgia and Virginia, and so through the city.

Next to the churches come the secret and beneficial
societies. The Colored Masons date from 1826; the Odd
Fellows own a four-story hall on Twenty-ninth Street,
where ninety-six separate societies meet and pay an annual rental of $5,000. Then there are old societies like
the African dating back to 1808, and new ones like the
Southern Beneficial with very large memberships. There
is a successful building association, a hospital, an orphan
asylum, and a home for the aged, all entirely conducted
by negroes, and mainly supported by them. Public en-
tertainments are continually provided by the various
churches and by associations such as the Railway Porters'
Union, the West Indian Benevolent Association, the Lincoln Literary, &c.

Here, then, is a world of itself, closed in from the outer world and almost unknown to it, with churches, clubs, hotels, saloons, and charities; with its own social distinctions, amusements, and ambitions. Its members are rarely rich, according to the standards of to-day. Probably less than ten negroes in New York own over $50,000 worth of property each, and the total property held may be roughly estimated as between three and four millions. Many homes have been bought in Brooklyn and the suburbs in the last ten years, so that there is a comfortable class of laborers.

The morality and education of this black world is naturally below that of the white world. That is the core of the negro problem. Nevertheless, it would be wrong to suppose here a mass of ungraded ignorance and lewdness. The social gradations toward the top are sharp and distinct, and the intelligence and good conduct of the better classes would pass muster in a New England village. As we descend the social distinctions are less rigid, and toward the bottom the great difficulty is to distinguish between the bad and the careless, the idle and the criminal, the unfortunate and the imposters.

PHILADELPHIA

From early times there was a steady northward flow of free negroes and fugitive slaves, and these immigrants invariably sought the cities. Thus we find the negro population concentrating and growing in the City of Philadelphia. At the time of the first census there were 2,500 negroes there, and a century later there were 40,000. To-day there are 62,613 negroes in Philadelphia —a population larger than that of the whole city when it was the capital of the Nation.

Practically then a study of the negro in Pennsylvania means a study of the metropolis of the State. We have here without doubt an interesting group of men. To-day if one visits Philadelphia one plainly sees that this city of 1,293,970 souls has a considerable number of black folk.

They live in the central part of Philadelphia—the historic Seventh Ward, while the main white residence districts have stretched northward toward Germantown and westward across the Schuylkill. The Seventh Ward was itself a residence section fifty years ago, and then the negroes were strictly confined to a ghetto bordering the Delaware River.

Gradually as they grew in numbers they moved up into the city. Finally in the last decade they have scattered more among the white population, moving northward in smaller numbers toward Germantown and southward toward the bay.

The Seventh Ward, however, is still their chief dwell-

ing place, its 10,000 negroes being more than a third of
its total population. It is an interesting sight of a Sun-
day morning to walk down Lombard Street, Philadelphia,
and watch this mass of people. Here the chief churches
and halls are situated. Here is the general promenade of
all classes and conditions.

Here one can see the Northern negro in a peculiar
way. They differ decidedly from the crowds of a
Southern city in dress and carriage, in their demeanor
toward the whites, and their general air of self-reliance.
They are well dressed and clean, and they have about
them a certain air of prosperity. The first question one
naturally asks is, How do they earn a living amid the
competition of a large Northern city?

The answer is of so much importance that a glance
into the past will best help us to understand it. When,
early in the last century, the negroes began to come to
Philadelphia they easily found there an assured economic
footing. By 1810 they formed nearly 16 per cent. of the
population, and did practically all the housework and
common labor and a good part of the work in the
mechanical trades. White mechanics had protested
against this, back in the eighteenth century, but it was
to the interest of the masters then to hire out slave
mechanics on good terms.

After emancipation, the negro mechanics lost this
protection, and a hard economic struggle in the trades
took place. The negroes were fairly successful in hold-
ing their own until outside forces began to tell. Philadelphia, feeling the influence of the industrial revolution
after the war of 1812, began to change from a provincial
capital to a great manufacturing centre. White mechanics

and laborers hurried to the city and far outnumbered the blacks.

Even then the negro mechanics might have held their own had it not been for the peculiar limitations which prejudice placed about them. Their better class could not rise above the mass. Public opinion placed the successful, law-abiding city negro along with the untrained and lazy immigrant. And when these immigrants began to sink into poverty and crime, public opinion turned against the negro, and he rapidly lost ground as an industrial factor.

About 1840 new obstacles appeared in the propaganda of the Abolitionists and the increased influx of foreign immigrants. The wrath of the pro-slavery party spent itself on the free negroes, and the new foreign workmen were not slow to use race prejudice as a means of shutting negroes almost entirely out of the new industries which were now arising on all sides. For ten years and more the negroes were repeatedly the object of mob violence, the right of suffrage was taken away, and the growth of the black population seriously checked.

To take away any considerable part of the customary livelihood of a mass of people means that their ingenuity will be stimulated to find new avenues of labor, if they are really energetic and resourceful. And the Philadelphia negroes were energetic. They had established their own churches and beneficial societies, they had accumulated some property, they had sent their children to school, and they were not willing to be simply and always servants and common laborers.

Led by a group of excellent business men they developed the catering business of Philadelphia to such an extent as to make it famous all over the land. This was a natural resource. They had among them numbers of well-trained servants. By serving several families instead of one, investing capital in table furniture, and adding taste and skill, there was evolved the negro caterer. He invented the business, conducted it without a rival for two generations, and only lost his pre-eminence when industrial changes after the war substituted the stock company for the individual undertaker of limited capital.

Moreover, after the war this group of negroes was again overwhelmed and almost submerged beneath a mass of immigrants from the freed masses of the South. How have they emerged from this crisis, and what do they do for a living to-day? The negroes of Philadelphia to-day are occupied about as follows:

	Per Cent.
Professions, (physicians, lawyers, clergymen, &c.)	1.5
Conducting business, (merchants, caterers, expressmen,) with their own capital	4.0
Artisans, (carpenters, masons, upholsterers, &c.)	8.5
Clerks and responsible workers, (cooks, stewards, messengers, managers, foremen, policemen, actors, &c.)	3.0
Laborers, select, (teamsters, janitors, stevedores, elevator men, hostlers, &c.)	12.0
Laborers, ordinary	32.0
Servants	39.0
Total	100.0

In other words, of the 63,000 negroes in Philadelphia, 37,500 actually work in gainful occupations. Of these at least 26,500 are servants and ordinary laborers, while 4,500 others are laborers of a little higher grade. Another 4,500 are clerks and artisans, while 2,000 are business and professional men.

The servants and laborers are composed mainly of the recent Southern born immigrants to the city. They find little else open to them, and only a few are fitted for other work. Some of them are artisans and they find some work in the building trades, and in a few large establishments, notably the Midvale Steel Works. For the most part, however, they are entirely shut out from mechanical labor by the trades unions, which in nearly all cases frankly or covertly debar the negro. The cigarmakers' union is almost the only exception.

The descendants of the free negroes and other Northern trained colored people, together with some of the best of the Southerners, have gone into business and professional lines. The openings in the large business firms for colored boys are very few. The business ventures by negroes are mostly small shops. The physicians are the most successful professional men.

A careful consideration of the ages of the members of any community and of the relative number of men and women always teaches the student something of the social conditions there. When we find a great many more men than women, as in the Western States, we know this is due to migration and unusual opportunities for work. So, too, an excess of children and old people in any place would indicate the migration of those in the prime of life to find work elsewhere.

Among the negroes of Philadelphia and of most large cities there is a marked excess of females and a preponderance of young people between the ages of twenty and thirty years. Sixty years ago the negro women of Philadelphia outnumbered the men more than three to two. To-day the proportion is a little less than six to five.

This is the result of open chances for young women to work as servants and restricted chances for young men. The age distribution shows that the young people of the South are hurrying Northward in search of large opportunities. Such a migration, however, has its dangers, for all experience shows that the ages of twenty and thirty are peculiarly a period of temptation to excess and crime.

Moreover, the negro home life is, on account of slavery, already weak, sending forth children poorly equipped to meet the allurements of a great city. The excess of young women further complicates the situation, so that under this peculiar moral and economic stress it is well to ask just how this population is standing the strain.

There is without doubt a great deal of crime among negroes. When any race passes through a vast and sudden change like that of emancipation from slavery the result is always that numbers unable to adjust themselves to the new circumstances easily sink into debauchery and crime. We should expect then to find the greatest excess of crime a generation after emancipation and then to see it gradually decrease to normal conditions.

This is partially exemplified in Philadelphia. The act of gradual emancipation did not begin to have full effect until about 1810. From 1829 to 1834 the negroes, who were less than 9 per cent. of the total population, committed 29 per cent. of the serious crime. This outbreak of crime among young negroes was met, not by efforts at regeneration and opportunities for betterment, but by repression, denunciation, and restricted openings. The result was that from 1835 to 1839 negroes committed over 40 per cent. of the serious crime, although they formed but 7½ per cent. of the population.

As the better class of negroes, however, continued diligently at work, conditions gradually grew better. By 1850 the negroes were charged with but 16 per cent. of the serious crime, and by 1874 less than 4 per cent. of the arrests in Philadelphia were arrests of colored persons. In other words, negro crime had become about normal.

Then came a change. The Centennial Exhibition was the beginning of a new immigration of negroes. They came from the South, and represented young people only a few years removed from slavery.

It must be expected that the percentage of criminals and social failures among such a class would be large. It was large. From 1876, and coincident with the influx of Southern immigrants, the percentage of crime for which negroes are responsible in Philadelphia has steadily risen from 4 per cent. to 9 per cent. To-day the negroes, forming one-twentieth of the population, commit about one-eleventh of the crime, judging by the crude measure of arrests.

While this is not nearly as bad as the record in the past, it is nevertheless a serious problem. It is not fair, of course, to charge Philadelphia negroes with this amount of crime without discrimination. We must remember that only a fifth of those committing the more serious crimes are Philadelphia-born, and three-fifths of them are immigrants from the South and the product of its peculiar social conditions.

The North has a direct interest in the race problem in the South, and cannot expect permanent improvement in the criminal rate of its negro population as long as

Southern conditions breed crime and send it North. At the same time the city itself is partially responsible.

Receiving, as it does, a population easily tempted to crime, it ought not to make yielding to temptation easier than honest labor. And yet, by political protection to criminals and indiscriminate charity, it encourages the worthless and at the same time, by shutting negroes out of most avenues of honest employment, the city discourages labor and thrift.

The fight for a livelihood and the temptation to crime are both a severe strain to physical health. It was a generation ago confidently asserted that Northern cities would never have a large negro population because of the cold climate and the stress of competition. The continued growth of this population afterward was laid solely to migration. This is only partially true.

The death rate of negroes in Philadelphia is higher than that of whites for obvious reasons. The majority live in the most unsanitary sections of the city, and in the worst houses in those sections; high rents lead to crowding, and ignorance of city life to unhealthful habits. As a consequence, the death rate of the negroes exceeds that of the whites just as the death rate of an unsanitary region exceeds that of a clean, orderly city.

In the decade 1820-30, the Negro death rate was over 47½ in every thousand; in 1830-40 it was 32½ in every thousand, against 24 for the whites. If, however, this difference in death rate is due solely to difference in conditions of life, we should expect an improvement in the death rate to-day as compared with the past, and a smaller death rate in the residence districts of the better class of negroes.

The death rate of the negroes has fallen from 47.6 per thousand in 1820-30, to 28.02 in 1891-96. Moreover, while the death rate in the slums of the Fifth Ward is 48½, in the better home life of the Thirtieth Ward it is practically the same as that of the whites, 21 per thousand. While then the high death rate of the negro is a misfortune to him and a menace to his neighbors, the evil is one which will easily yield to the influence of cleaner streets, better houses, and better homes.

Looking now at the social conditions of this mass of 60,000 souls, we are first struck by the fact that a rapid differentiation into social classes is going on. The common measure of this would be that of accumulated property.

There are no rich negroes according to the standards of modern wealth. Indeed, the income of a people who find the problem of breadwinning so difficult would preclude this. These incomes are something like this:

EARNINGS PER WEEK PER FAMILY.

	P.C.		P.C.
$5 or less	18	$10 to $15	26
$5 to $10	48	$15 or over	8

The negroes are earning to-day as a mass probably more than formerly. From these small incomes they have accumulated property as follows:

1821	$281,162	1855	$2,685,693
1838	322,532	1898	5,000,000
1848	531,809		

Only one negro is reputed to be worth over $100,000. Four have estates worth from $50,000 to $100,000; eleven, $25,000 to $50,000, and thirty-seven from

$10,000 to $25,000. One obstacle to saving is the high
rent which negroes are compelled to pay for houses.
Over $1,250,000 are annually spent for rent by this
race, and the rents paid are from 10 to 30 per cent.
higher than whites pay.

The average monthly rent per family is $10.50.
Twenty-two per cent. of the families pay less than $5
a month; the mass, or 57 per cent., pay between $10
and $20. The result of high rents is crowding, so that
through a system of sub-letting fully a third of the
families in one of the most populous wards live in one-
room apartments.

If in addition to economic differences we bring in
considerations of education and morals we may divide
the colored people of Philadelphia, roughly, into four
classes. The lowest class are the slum elements—criminals, gamblers, and loafers who form the "submerged
Tenth." They live in the alleys of the older ward,
centre about "clubs" and near saloons, and form, perhaps, 6 per cent. or more of the city negro population.
They are a dangerous class both to their own people and
to the whites, are responsible for much serious crime,
and tempt the hardworking immigrants from the South
into excess and immorality.

Above these come the poor and unfortunate. They
are the class of negroes who for various reasons have not
succeeded in the sharp competition of city life. They include unfortunates who want work and cannot find it,
good-natured but unreliable workmen who cannot keep
work, hand workers who spend regularly more than they
earn, and in general people poor but not criminal nor
grossly immoral. Thirty per cent. of the negroes would

probably fall in this class.

Above these would be the bulk of the laborers—hard-working, good-natured people, not as pushing and re-sourceful as some, but honest and faithful, of fair and rapidly improving morals, and with some education. Fifty-two per cent. of the negroes fall into this class. Their chief difficulty is in finding paying employment outside of menial service.

Finally about 12 per cent. of the negroes form an aristo-cracy of wealth and education. They correspond to the better middle-class population of modern cities, and have, usually, good common-school training, with here and there a high school or college man. They occupy comfortable homes, are educating their children, and own property.

They, too, have difficulty in finding careers for their children, and they are socially in an anomalous position. The world classes them with the mass of their race, and even in a city like Philadelphia makes but little allow-ance for their culture or means. On the other hand, not being to any considerable extent themselves employers of colored labor, or bound to them by ties of industrial interest, they cannot easily assume leadership over their own people. Indeed, a natural instinct of self-defense and self-preservation drives them away from the lower masses of their people.

They feel that they can only maintain their position and advance further by drawing social lines against the incompetent and criminal of their own race. Thus they face a peculiar paradox, and stand between black and white, the representatives of all that is best in the one and at the same time suffering vicariously at the hands of the other for all that is worst among their own people.

BOSTON

Slavery in Massachusetts began with the undoing of the Pequods in 1638 and the sailing of the slaver Desire about the same time. At the beginning of the eighteenth century there were 400 negroes in Boston. A century later there were 1,200.

At the beginning of the twentieth century there were 12,000 negroes in Boston. The growth of this population was slow and steady until 1850, when it increased more quickly. Since 1880 it has grown rapidly.

The negroes from the first were house servants almost exclusively, and the comparatively small demand for these in a thoroughly democratic community early put a stop to further importation. The presence of those already there, however, was as puzzling as in other Colonies.

James Otis declared slavery inconsistent with the principles of the Revolution, and it certainly seemed so after the songs of Phillis Wheatly and the bold fighting of black men at Bunker Hill. Nevertheless, even early emancipation did not secure equal rights for negroes.

After the Revolution negroes complained that in the streets of Boston they were "shamefully abused," and that to such a degree that "we may truly be said to carry our lives in our hands." They were for some time taxed without having the right of suffrage. Separate schools were maintained until 1855. Intermarriage of the races was forbidden until 1843, and as late as the civil war often "large audiences have been thrown almost into spasms by the presence of one colored man."

The 12,000 negroes of Boston to-day are largely immigrants since the war, as the excess of adults shows. Nevertheless, this urban negro population is peculiar in being the only one among the larger Northern cities to have a normal distribution of the sexes—5,904 males and 5,687 females in 1900.

This immediately leads us to expect better family life and social conditions than we have yet studied. Thanks to Massachusetts schools, the illiteracy of this group is about that of England and France, (13½ per cent.)

The oldest colored settlement was on the north side of Beacon Hill, in the West End. For a century and more this has been the historic centre of the blacks. Here was the African meeting house, where the anti-slavery movement was launched, here was the first negro school, and here still are the chief churches and halls. The bulk of the population, however, has moved.

By 1860 this district had become crowded and congested, and by 1870 the influx of low characters made the problem of home life among the better class of negroes as difficult as it is in the New York "Tenderloin" of to-day.

Even as late as 1880 it was very difficult for a negro to rent or buy a house outside this district. Gradually, however, the newer tenement houses of the South End, beyond the Common and out Tremont Street, were hired and purchased. To-day some 4,000 or 5,000 negroes live there, leaving perhaps 2,500 still in the vicinity of Joy Street, and many are scattered in the little settlements between.

It is, however, in the purchase of pretty suburban homes scattered here and there throughout the towns surrounding Boston that the negroes have been peculiarly successful in solving the problem of living. Since the marvelous development of Boston's street car service thousands of the better class of negroes have bought homes in Cambridge, Roxbury, Dorchester, and Chelsea, and other places.

These settlements are not usually in colonies, but the black families are scattered here and there among the whites, and the opposition which black neighbors at first aroused has largely died away, save, I believe, in the aristocratic suburb of Brookline.

It was always thought pretty certain that Boston would have no considerable negro population on account of the high death rate. Early in the eighteenth century the negro deaths for ten years averaged 87 per 1,000, and during ten years in the middle of the century it was 73. By the middle of the nineteenth century the rate had, however, fallen to 40, and since the war it has steadily decreased. The following table will illustrate this:

	Death Rate Per 1,000.	
	Whites.	Negroes.
1875	23	31
1880	23	33
1885	24	42
1890	23	32
1895	23	30
1900	20	25

Economic conditions in Boston also show considerable difference from those in the other cities. The different environment, the less eager rush for wealth, and the New

England ideals of home and society have plainly influenced the negroes. Of those who work for a living only 60 per cent., a little over half, are servants and ordinary laborers—less than half of the men, and three-fourths of the working women. This is an unusually small proportion for a negro population. At the same time, it renders the negro a relatively unimportant part of the common labor force of Boston.

In Boston as elsewhere the typical negro employments are disappearing. The negro waiter is going from the hotels. The negro barber is disappearing. The negro bootblack has almost gone.

Ordinary observers have supposed that this displacement leaves no work for negroes. This is true in the sense that there are few employments now which are his by right and common consent. As long as there were such employments they fell under the stigma of race prejudice and they failed to attract the best talent of the negroes—hence negro waiters who were poor, careless barbers, and the like. To-day as these employments are open to all the negro is pushing as a competitor into higher walks.

In New York and Philadelphia the negro is too largely handicapped by race prejudice to make much headway, but he has made some. In Boston the atmosphere has been more liberal, although by no means unbiased, and he has had correspondingly better success. The select laborers, as janitors, porters, messengers, draymen, &c., are an unusually trustworthy and respectable class in Boston. They form perhaps 15 per cent. of the workers, and they are connecting links between menial labor and skilled labor or business.

In the skilled trades there are about 15 per cent. of the colored workers, chiefly barbers, dressmakers, railway employes, tailors, carpenters, masons, painters, &c. In the mechanical industries which fill East Boston and South Boston there are few negroes, although large concerns like the American Tool and Machine Company have a few colored apprentices.

There are quite a number of negroes in the building trades, and they work side by side with whites on some jobs. Often they work for colored contractors. The negro tailors are well represented and very skillful.

In the various lines of business enterprise will be found about 7 per cent. of the colored people. This includes merchants, peddlers, clerks, salesmen, agents, &c. Among the leading merchants are:

Five merchant tailors, with a trade of $20,000 to $50,000 a year.

Three undertakers, with a trade of $5,000 to $10,000 a year.

Five caterers, with a trade of $5,000 to $25,000 a year.

Four real estate dealers, with a trade of $5,000 to $10,000 a year.

Besides these there are two tobacconists, a florist, a butcher, and a bookdealer, who do considerable business. The tailors and real estate men are most successful. The chief of the former conducts a large and well-known establishment on Washington Street. The real estate men have made money in supplying the demand for better homes, especially in the suburbs.

The caterers are also to be noticed. They are not here, as in Philadelphia, the last of a noted guild, but are instances of individual push. One conducted a fashionable suburban hotel until the crash of 1892. After losing this, he pluckily started again and now has another suburban inn and a large city restaurant. He is the inventor of a bread machine which the Bread Trust hopes to use.

Much more frequently than in the other two cities, Boston negroes have gained positions in large mercantile establishments. Yet here the black boy's chance of promotion is nothing like the white boy's. The son of a prominent negro, who had been graduated from a college of the first rank and had some capital of his own, wished a place in a mercantile establishment to learn business methods. He was promised several openings, but at last all frankly told him that their employes objected, and they could not take him.

He nevertheless went into business for himself, and is to-day very successful. Usually the positions gained are by reason of long service as a laborer. A porter in a shoe store has recently been made head of the stock department, but it took him fifteen years to gain this promotion.

A large bicycle firm has put a negro in charge of its repairing department. One of the largest furniture stores has a black floor walker. A wholesale clothing house has a colored salesman. An East Boston shipbuilder has a negro draughtsman. Notman, the Photographer, has a black assistant.

And there are instances of negroes employed as chemists, druggists, architects, and engravers. Some half-dozen stenographers hold good positions—one in the general office of the Fitchburg Railroad. In a few cases business men have taken bright bell boys and servants out of hotels and given them a chance in their stores. The pity is that ability, when hidden by color, is so seldom sought out and put to use!

A little less than 3 per cent. of the Boston negroes are in the professions and Government service. There are twelve negro lawyers, and nowhere else in the country, save in Chicago, are colored lawyers so successful. One is a Master in Chancery, and at least seven have a practice of $5,000 or more annually.

Their clients are largely white foreigners. One negro held the position of Judge in the Charleston Court some years ago, but is now dead.

Among the medical men in Boston are nine general practitioners, four dentists, and one veterinary surgeon. Five of these make large incomes. One of the dentists was formerly a demonstrator in Harvard University and is one of the finest dentists in Boston, having many of the best families of the city among his patrons.

There are always a considerable number of negro students in Boston—six or eight in Harvard College, a number in the professional school, in Boston University, the Institute of Technology, and the public high schools.

The chief political positions held in Boston by negroes are a Deputy Collector of Taxes, a Deputy Sealer of Weights and Measures, a Deputy Sheriff, a Postmaster of a city sub-station, and a Sergeant of Police. Through the civil service competitive examinations considerable numbers have secured appointments in the postal service and the city civil service.

In Boston and the immediate suburbs there is one Principal of a public school with white teachers and pupils, and there are five colored teachers in various other schools. In the governing bodies of the city and vicinity are two Aldermen and three Common Councilmen.

There have been several colored members of the Legislature and one negro in the Governor's Council. One of the Aldermen mentioned was formerly the famous black class orator at Harvard in 1890. He has made an excellent record as a public servant.

It is noticeable that only 62 per cent. of the Boston negroes are in gainful occupations, a smaller proportion than in the other cities, showing a larger number of children in school and a larger number of mothers and daughters making and keeping homes. There are no very wealthy negroes in Boston, but a large number of persons owning homes worth from $2,000 to $10,000.

There are in Boston a half dozen estates of $25,000 or more, ten or fifteen from $10,000 to $25,000, belonging to negroes. Their total wealth is probably between two and three millions of dollars.

It would be wrong to suppose that beneath the fair conditions described there was not the usual substratum of crime and idleness. Seventy years ago the negroes of Massachusetts furnished 14 per cent. of the convicts. Just before the war they still furnished 11 per cent., although forming less than 1 per cent. of the population.

To-day, forming 2 per cent. of the population, they furnish 2¼ per cent. of the prisoners, 3½ per cent. of the penitentiary convicts, and 1½ per cent. of the paupers. While not ideal, this record is very encouraging.

On the whole Boston negroes are more hopeful than those in New York and Philadelphia. A prominent negro

author said recently in The Boston Globe, in answer to
the question "Do negroes expect to attain perfect
equality with the whites?"

Contrast the changes which have taken place here during
the last half century in relation to this question. What have
we to-day in place of all that inequality and wrong?

Complete equality before the law, in the public schools,
at the polls, and in public conveyances, and substantial
equality in hotels, restaurants, and places of amusement,
while on that self-same common from which colored boys
were once driven by what seemed at the time a relentless
race prejudice stands one of the noblest monuments of
genius in America, erected to commemorate the heroic serv-
ices to the Union of a regiment of black troops in the War
of the Rebellion.

SOME CONCLUSIONS

We have followed in some detail the history and condition of the colored people in the three chief cities of the Northeast, and there are some manifest conclusions which may here be gathered up and considered.

And first, in regard to the inner life of the negroes, it is apparent that we have been dealing with two classes of people, the descendants of the Northern free negroes and the freed immigrants from the South. This distinction is not always clear, as these two elements have mingled often so as to obliterate nearly all differences.

Yet it has everywhere been manifest in the long run that while a part of the negroes were native-born and trained in the culture of the city, the others were immigrants largely ignorant and unused to city life. There were, of course, manifold exceptions, but this was the rule. Thus the history of the negro in Northern cities is the history of the rise of a small group growing by accretions from without, but at the same time periodically overwhelmed by them and compelled to start again when once the new material had been assimilated.

Philadelphia is perhaps the best example of this. Four times the freed men started forward and four times they were overwhelmed and dragged back by a mass of immigrants. The first two times the newcomers were gradually incorporated and the group started with renewed energy.

Before the negroes, however, had recovered from the

invasion of 1876 the new stream of 1890 started and has not yet stopped, although the native-born Philadelphia negroes constitute but little over a quarter of the colored population. In New York the native-born have been perhaps even more completely overwhelmed. In Boston alone have they held their own sufficiently to retain considerable influence in the leadership of the group.

To realize what this cleft in the black world means we must remember that, as has been said, to all intents and purposes, the negroes form a world among themselves. They are so organized as to come in contact with the outer world as seldom as possible.

The average negro to-day knows the white world only from afar. His family and relatives are colored, his neighbors with few exceptions are colored, and his acquaintances are chiefly colored. He works with colored people, if not for them; he calls on colored people, attends meetings and joins societies of colored people, and goes to a colored church.

He reads the daily paper just as the whites read foreign news, chiefly for its facts relating to his interests; but for intimate local and social notes he reads The Age or The Tribune or The Courant—colored sheets. The chances are to-day that he is served by a colored physician, consults now and then a colored lawyer, and perhaps buys some of his supplies of colored merchants.

Thus the white world becomes to him only partially real, and then only at the points where he actually comes in contact with it—on the street car, in taking his employer's directions, and in a few of his amusements. This contact is least in New York and broadest in Boston, where it extends to restaurants, theatres, and churches.

Now there arises from such facts as these a peculiarly baffling question: Ought the black man to be satisfied with and encourage this arrangement, or should he be dissatisfied? In either case what ought he to do?

From the earliest times the attitude of the free negroes has been opposed to any organization or segregation of negroes as such. Men like Fortune, McCune, Smith, and Remond insisted that they were American citizens, not negroes, and should act accordingly. On the other hand, the Southern immigrants had of necessity been used to herding together. When they came North the clan spirit prevailed, partly from instinct, chiefly because they felt their company was not desired and they dreaded refusals and rebuffs.

The free negroes deeply resented this action; they declared it was voluntarily drawing the color line; that it showed cowardice, and that wherever the negro withdrew his pretensions to being treated as a man among men, he lost ground and made himself a pariah. Notwithstanding all this opposition the new immigrants organized, slowly but surely, the best and only defense of the ostracized against prejudice. They built negro churches, organized negro societies, settled in negro neighborhoods, and hired out to work in gangs.

They made a negro world and then in turn taunted the free negroes with wishing to escape from themselves, and being ashamed of their race and lineage. Here stood the paradox, and here it still stands to puzzle the best negro thought. How can negroes organize for social and economic purposes and not by that very organizing draw and invite the drawing of the color line? Every inpouring of freed Southern immigrants into the North has naturally forced their ideas of clan life on the community of blacks, estranged the older free negro element, and deprived the whole group of its best natural leadership.

The Northern negro needs to-day intelligent, far-seeing leadership. His problem differs from the problems in the South, because his history, condition, and environment are different. And such leadership demands leisure for thought and education—the emerging again of a dominant intelligent class such as the free negroes formerly were. This would rapidly happen could the negro find work.

The problem of work, the problem of poverty, is to-day the central, baffling problem of the Northern negro. It is useless and wrong to tell the negro to stay South where he can find work. A certain sort of soul, a certain kind of spirit, finds the narrow repression and provincialism of the South simply unbearable. It sends the aspiring white man North, it sends also the negro. It is a natural movement and should not be repressed.

And yet the surest way to pervert the movement and ruin good immigrants and encourage criminals is the policy of refusing negroes remunerative work. That this is the case at present all evidence proves; the evidence of strain in domestic relations as shown by late marriage, deserted wives, children out of school, and unhealthful homes. Such strain falling as it does on the weakest spot in the negro's social organization—the home—is a partial explanation of idleness and crime, while the encouragement of professional criminals and gamblers in our large cities furnishes whatever additional explanation is needed.

Turning now to the white population of these cities, it is probably true that the larger part of them are aware of no particular desire to hinder the progress of negroes. The question is one of mere academic interest to them, belonging principally, they imagine, to the South, and in regard to which they have inherited most of their opinions from their fathers. In practice they seldom meet negroes, know little of them, and are quite indifferent to them.

Then there is a large class of people who dislike negroes, and still others with positive views as to the natural inferiority of this branch of the human family. Further than this there are numbers of people who have a direct pecuniary interest in color discrimination—skilled workmen, who can thus further limit the supply for the labor market; clerks, salesmen, and managers, who fear for the dignity and respectability of their positions, and merchants and dealers, who dare not offend the public prejudice.

It is plain that with negative indifference, positive prejudice, and some pecuniary interests against the negro, and with simply a general humanitarian feeling on the part of a few for him, it is easy to make his opportunities narrow and his life burdensome. There can be no reasonable doubt but that the Northern negro receives less wages for his work and pays more rent for worse houses than white workmen, and that it is not altogether a matter of fitness that confines his work chiefly to common labor and menial service.

That the question of fitness plays a considerable part in determining the condition of the negro is without doubt true. His training hitherto has but ill-fitted him for the stern competition of world-city life. He knows but little of modern skilled labor, he has not been trained in thrift, he is not as a rule neat and tidy, and he is apt to be slow and unreliable.

True as this is of the mass everybody knows personally of individual exceptions to the rule. Even the most prejudiced admit this. If this be so then the only thing that the best interests of the black race and of the Nation demand is that these exceptions be treated as their deserts entitle them—that the energetic, resourceful black man, the thrifty, neat black woman, the negro carpenter, tanner, and steel worker, the boy of promise and the man of education be given that chance to make a living and enjoy life which America offers freely to every race and people except those whom she has most cruelly wronged.

Nor is this merely a matter of sentiment. To keep down the black men who are fit to rise costs the city something to-day and will cost more to-morrow. The black population of the North is growing. Despite the phenomenal increase in the white North the black North has silently kept abreast or been but little behind. It has doubtless increased more rapidly than the native whites and is still growing.

There can be no doubt of the drift of the black South northward. It is said that the Wilmington riot alone sent a thousand negroes to Philadelphia. Every failure of the South, every oppressive act, every unlawful excess shifts the black problem northward.

Many who see the cloud coming have thought that passive if not active discouragement of negroes might keep them away. The census figures do not bear them out in this. But what the census figures, taken in conjunction with the statistics of crime and the history of municipal misgovernment, do prove is this: That the exclusion of honest negro workmen from earning a living in the North means direct encouragement to the Northward migration of negro criminals and loafers.

The crime of negroes in New York is not natural or normal. It is the crime of a class of professional negro criminals, gamblers, and loafers, encouraged and protected by political corruption and race prejudice. The only sort of negro that is generously encouraged in Philadelphia is the criminal and the pauper.

The black man who wants charity or protection in crime in the Quaker City can easily get it. But the black man who wants work will have to tramp the pavements many a day. Thus crime is encouraged, politics corrupted, energy and honesty discredited, and a reception prepared for simple-minded negro immigrants such as Dunbar has so darkly painted in his "Sport of the Gods."

What is the remedy? First, the negroes must try to make the deserving and fit among them as numerous as possible. So long as the majority are mediocre workmen, and a considerable minority lazy and unreliable, those who seek to attack the race will have ample ammunition. Whatever, therefore, may be best as to negro organization in many lines, certainly all must unite in keeping the blacks from succumbing to the present temptations of city life. Three lines of effort here seem advisable: First, systematic search for work; second, better homes; third, political reform.

There must be no idleness. Work, even if poorly paid and menial, is better than no work. Rebuffs and refusals,

though brutal and repeated, should not discourage negroes from continually and systematically seeking a
chance to do their best.

Homes in respectable districts and healthful places
should be had. No respectable negro family should linger
a week in the Tenderloin of New York or the Fifth Ward
of Philadelphia, or in the worst parts of the West End in
Boston.

Concerted, organized effort can bring relief here, even
if it costs something in comfort and rent. The home
training of children should be more strict even than
that of whites. Social distinctions should be observed.
A rising race must be aristocratic; the good cannot consort with the bad—nor even the best with the less good.

Negroes have an interest in honest government. They
should not allow a few minor offices to keep them from
allying themselves with the reform movements in city
government. The police riot of New York is but one
clear proof of this.

Finally the white people of these three great cities
should [do their part]—but is it necessary here in the
twentieth century to point out so plain a duty to fair-
minded Americans?